# PRESIDENTIAL CONVERSATIONS

George S. Corey

New York

Published by Metabook, an imprint of Metabook Entertainment.


Metabook Inc.
375 Greenwich Street
New York, New York 10013
www.metabookentertainment.com


ISBN 978-0-9992119-0-8

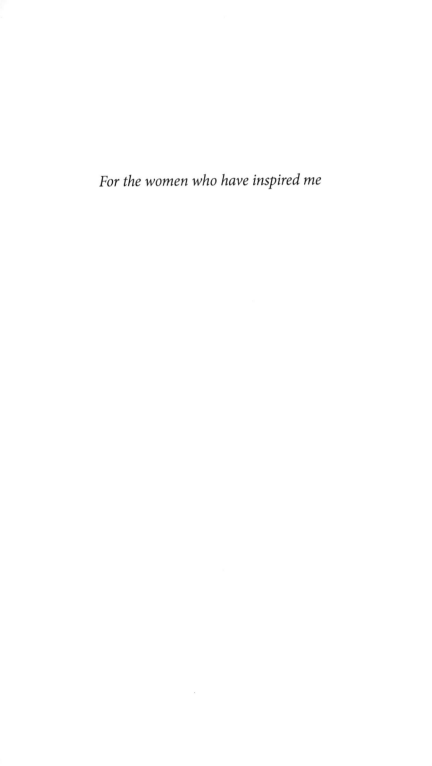

*For the women who have inspired me*

# CONTENTS

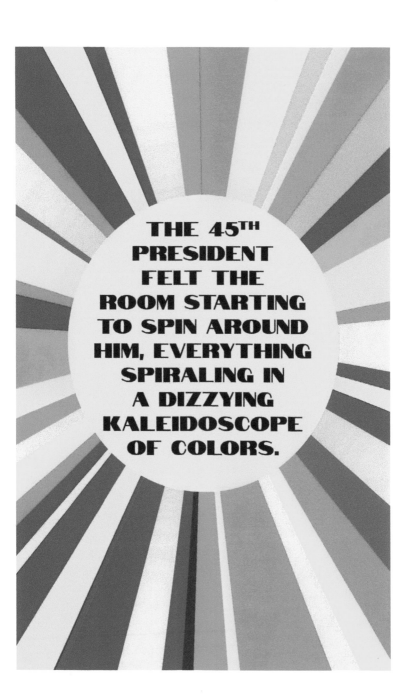

PRESIDENTIAL CONVERSATIONS

TRUMP

# PROLOGUE

n the wee hours of June 19, 2020, President Donald J. Trump slumped over his desk in the Oval Office, downright despondent about the rash of misfortunes which had overtaken his presidency. It was Juneteenth, but it might as well have been Friday the 13th for Trump. It was less than five months until the November 3 presidential election, and for the first time since he moved into the White House, he was scared.

Up until this moment, he'd always assumed his re-election was assured. Now, he was astonished to see his Democratic opponent, former vice president Joe Biden, well ahead of him in the polls; continued fallout from the Covid-19 crisis; and Black Lives Matter protests in the streets of every major city in America—including right in front of 1600 Pennsylvania Avenue in Washington, D.C.

Throughout his life, Trump had been extraordinarily adept at escaping his nemeses—lawsuits, bankruptcies, impeachment, the media—so to lose the presidency to "Sleepy Joe" Biden would be, for him, the ultimate public humiliation. The prospect left him shaken to the core.

Trump wasn't even in the mood to tweet.

He wondered where he could turn for solace. There was no one in his Cabinet or on his staff he trusted enough to turn to at the moment. He decided to call Steve Bannon first thing in the morning. Bannon would know what to do. But what could he do *now*? the president wondered. He had the shakes.

During the turbulent Watergate days of his presidency, Richard Nixon drank heavily and would sometimes discuss his tribulations with portraits of past presidents on the White House walls. But alcohol wasn't an option for the teetotalling Trump. And he certainly wasn't about to start talking to the walls!

There may have been some prescription Adderall in the medicine cabinet. But that wouldn't have helped, either. Unlike John F. Kennedy, who enjoyed marijuana (and perhaps LSD) in the White House with one of his mistresses, Trump was never intrigued by mind-altering drugs. For him, *power* was the greatest high—a natural high. And there was no pill to take for that.

In times like these, Trump often consulted with his wife. But the most recent Mrs. Trump, First Lady Melania, was fast asleep—and her beauty sleep was *not* to be disturbed. His first wife, Ivana, wasn't taking his calls. That left sweet little Marla—Marla Maples, his second wife. At least she hadn't shut him out entirely.

In fact, since their rather ugly tabloid divorce in 1999, Marla had deeply embraced spirituality as a lifestyle and had taken to sending him "spiritual care packages"—yoga tapes, scented candles, even healing crystals…never books.

Spirituality wasn't exactly Trump's thing, but Marla persisted. She wanted him to bring up his "love level" she'd tell him. *What the hell does that mean?* he wondered to himself.

In one of Marla's recent packages, along with a lipstick-smacked note in which she encouraged him to be "the best version of yourself," Marla had once again included a DVD of the music video for her song *The Pearl*. She'd sent it to him before, but he'd never watched it. Tonight, though, Trump was willing to try anything to ease his anxiety.

So, he told one of his military aides to tend to the TVs in the Oval Office, turn *off* the cable news channels and set up Marla's disc. Still in a suit, he took off his jacket, loosened his red tie and fell back in his chair. He reached for a sip of Diet Coke and thumbed PLAY on the remote control.

And there was Marla! Singing, or at least ably lip-synching, while standing atop a mountain. Her white dress billowed about her as she stretched her arms out like Jesus'. She looked like an angel. A New Age Angel. Now she looked like she was underwater! Trump was transfixed. There was "the look" she used to give him when they were together! And suddenly, it felt like the '90s again!

Trump relaxed into a smile, as he thought back to his "old life," before all this political business. Back to a time when he was the King of New York City—or at least Atlantic City—and the Czar of Reality TV. His hair looked *even better* in those days. *Aaahhh…*Nirvana. The peak sensation.

Trump turned up the volume. As Marla cooed and swayed to the mystical beat, Trump was enveloped by psychedelic swirls in the most vibrant yellows, pinks, purples and greens. The 45th president felt the room starting to spin around him, everything spiraling in a dizzying kaleidoscope of colors.

*What is happening?* he wondered. Whatever it was, he liked it! It felt *groovy*. He felt like a god atop Mount Olympus—not like the president with the cratering approval rating. He was floating!

Then, without warning, THUD. It all came to a cruel and sudden stop.

Trump looked around him. Nothing but silence. Whatever had just happened was only the beginning of Trump's strangest night on Earth, one which would see him visited by a parade of past presidents—and possibly change the course of history.

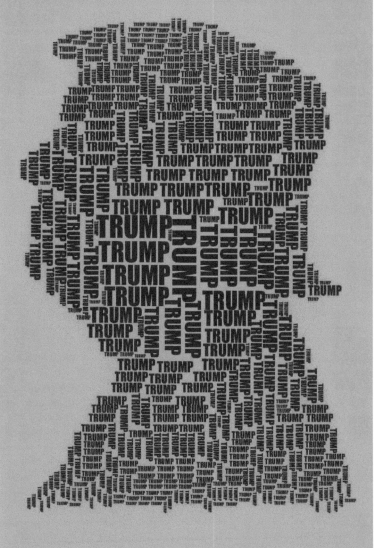

**PRESIDENTIAL CONVERSATIONS**

# WASHINGTON

# THE GENERAL

George Washington, naturally, was the first to visit President Trump in the Oval Office. A chorus of unseen trumpets regally heralded him, and *Poof!* —he materialized from a multicolored haze right there on the presidential seal. Washington was already shaking his head in admonishment.

"Mr. Trump, I understand you have an issue with truthfulness," said the first president. "What is this I hear about your uttering more than 20,000 falsehoods—*so far*—in your presidency?!"

Trump wasn't spooked by this strange apparition. On the contrary, he was tickled that America's first president was visiting him from the great unknown.

"Wow, this is just great!" exclaimed Trump. "I guess everyone's eyes are fixed on me, even up in heaven—or wherever you're from. But seriously?! *You* are lecturing *me* about truth?! You wanna talk about truth, Washington?! Can I call you George? You know, I heard that the cherry tree story was totally made up!"

Washington, smiling amiably said, "Sir, I am delighted that you are going to spar with me, because, admittedly, the afterlife is lovely if a bit dull for an old general."

Washington continued, "Yes, that apocryphal story was spread by one of my own supporters! But I always tried to be truthful, and that is why I am speaking with you today. It was my reputation for truthfulness and sincerity that helped me as our nation's first supreme general and our first president and commander in chief."

Trump's white-ringed eyes narrowed with skepticism.

"You appear unconvinced," said Washington. "Let me then describe one of my speeches wherein my reputation for honesty was paramount. Perhaps you are familiar with my Newburgh Address?"

"Doesn't ring a bell," shrugged Trump.

"It is from the year 1783, before my presidency. Can you imagine, President Trump, that a speech actually prevented a near mutiny by my own generals? And this was after we had beaten the British!

"You see, my good sir, my generals were unhappy because the Continental Congress had failed to provide them with the back pay that was owed to them, in addition to their pensions, for their service to our country during the American Revolution. The generals were justifiably angry, and they were ready to revolt!

"I infiltrated their secret meeting, about which they were none too happy. And to get their attention, I walked to the head of the hall, careful not to make eye contact and risk further enflaming their hostility. I reached into my waistcoat pocket, drew out my spectacles, and held them before me. I carefully unfolded the ingenious little mechanism for all to see, which drew their attention and quieted the room's grumblings. Just the sight of my balancing the spectacles on my nose silenced my generals; none thought their invincible commander would let himself appear old or weak. But I told them, 'Gentlemen, you will permit me to put on my spectacles, for I have not only grown gray but almost blind in the service of my country.'"

Trump squinted, then sarcastically replied, "Really? That's it?! You put your glasses on and saved the country, is that what you're telling me?"

"Verily, it was so, Mr. President," nodded Washington excitedly. "But it was not the mere act of donning my spectacles, it was the words I chose with which to deliver my message. When my generals saw that I had opened myself to their pity and ridicule, they were deeply moved and listened intently. And at the end, my words of assurance allowed me more time to lobby Congress to get my generals and our troops paid, which I did accomplish."

Trump scoffed at this, saying, "I would have projected power, and come in with my elite troops, guns blazing, rather than beg to anyone."

"I am truly enjoying myself with some of your brash modern ways!" said Washington. Then he fixed such a stare on the 45th commander in chief that Trump stepped back. "But I admonish such remarks in the strongest terms and impart this lesson—that you cannot lead at the point of a sword or muzzle of a rifle, but only by honorable words and deeds."

Trump could not help himself, and remarked, "Whoa, Georgie! I get it! I'm all about honor. But you gotta understand, there are a lotta swamp dwellers polluting our great capital these days. *A lot.*"

Trump then darted his eyes to the top of Washington's head and blurted out, "Hey, you're my height! You must have been a giant in your day!"

"Indeed, it was so," said Washington.

"Very important," Trump replied. "People do not like to have a short president."

Washington sighed. "I will sum up with a final lesson to you, Mr. President, from my Farewell Address at the end of my presidency," he said. "I warned the young nation, legislators and citizens alike, that we as a people must have unity at home and independence abroad to remain strong."

"That's what my presidency stands for, too!" Trump interjected. "*Making America Great Again* at home and making the rest of the world respect our strength and power again. Maybe even fear us."

"I ask you to listen," said Washington, again fixing the president with his steely gaze. "This very moment is the reason I am visiting with you, and this is my sole chance to get through to you.

"At my Farewell Address, I spoke of the need for national unity and for denouncing excessive partisanship—especially in the form of political parties—as I believed a party system would ultimately tear the country asunder."

GEORGE!
GEORGE!
GEORGE!

"Georgie, I gotta tell you, you're not being realistic," said Trump. "First of all, it was much easier for you because you were 'the great general.' And second, after your presidency, every election in this country has been partisan. And every American president after you has had to divide and conquer.

"And I've actually done a great job uniting the country—*my part* of the country."

"I now fully understand that convincing you, Mr. President, would be a long campaign and, indeed, it may very well mean that many other presidents will need to visit you," said Washington gravely. "But I am determined to do my part. And so, in terms of your foreign policy, I must warn you against foreign entanglements.

"In my time, it was Great Britain and France and the European powers that threatened my young nation. And right here on American soil, many British loyalists would have welcomed back the dangers, excesses and unchecked power of a monarchy.

"When the Constitution of the United States was written, it was with the full knowledge that I would be the first president. It was known that it would be left to me to decide whether to be the first citizen of my fellow citizens or the first king over my fellow citizens."

Washington stepped closer. "Know that it was in my power to make myself a king," he said quietly.

"In my opinion, you blew it, Georgie," Trump said, shaking his head. "I'll never understand how you or any man could turn his back on making himself a king! Or how you walked away after only two

*TRUTH* by Cleo

terms as president when you could have made yourself president for life!

"Are they familiar with the term 'winner' up there in heaven?" Trump asked. "Because that's not what you sound like here!

"And Georgie, do you know I just visited Mount Vernon? I couldn't understand why you didn't put your name anywhere. My name is on everything I do. TRUMP Tower. TRUMP Plaza. The TRUMP Organization. I've even got people calling my private jet TRUMP Force One! It says to the world *Here I Am*—usually in big, shiny gold letters. To everyone! All around the world."

"Yes, about that," Washington sighed. "Mr. President, I implore you to try to seek a better understanding about the dangers of your foreign entanglements."

"Such as?" Trump simpered.

"Well," replied Washington, "Russia, for instance and your dealings with Mr. Putin. Or, eh, Ukraine?"

"Fake news!" stammered Trump. "Vladimir Putin is a terrific person. And my call with President Zelensky was perfect! Ask anybody."

"Mr. President, I implore you to understand that it was only my blunt truthfulness, at home and abroad, and my willingness to step down from power, that gave strength to actions. I can only hope that by explaining to you how I lived, with a life of honesty, civility and sincerity, that I have inspired you to embrace these same traits in an attempt to unify and strengthen our great nation. But I fear you have not taken heed of my words."

Trump then dismissed The Father of His Country with a little wave. "Okay, that's enough," he said. "Bye-bye, Georgie. I'll think of you whenever I see a one-dollar bill, which I can tell you isn't very often." Grumbling under his breath, Trump said, "I'm going to put *my* face on the $10,000 bill!"

And with that, the first president vanished from Trump's Oval Office.

**PRESIDENTIAL CONVERSATIONS**

JEFFERSON

# THE SCRIBE

resident Trump looked around him, saying "Okay, bring it, who's next? President number two? Who was that…Benjamin Franklin?!"

Thomas Jefferson scurried in, twirling his favorite quill, saying "No, no, Mr. President, *c'est moi!*"

Trump scoffed, "Jefferson! You always loved the French more than your own country. So, you were the second president, huh? I knew that."

"*Monsieur le Président*, my longtime competitor and sometimes foe, John Adams, was 'president number two' and he was one of the best men to serve in this role. Unfortunately for you, he has declined to speak with you at this time on account of his lovely and accomplished wife, Abigail, how shall I say, quite detesting you…"

Jefferson continued buoyantly, "But I, the *third* president, came most willingly to discuss my presidency. You must be familiar with my finest accomplishment, The Declaration of Independence?"

"Oh, yeah! It's a great document, Tom, just fantastic," chimed Trump.

"Indeed, it is a work of such far-reaching vision, it may never be equaled," Jefferson said in a tone of great satisfaction.

"Well, I don't know about that," Trump retorted.

Waving his favorite quill theatrically, Jefferson said, "If you will indulge me, my favorite phrase in the Declaration has become the most beloved."

*We hold these truths to be self-evident, that all men are created equal, that they are endowed by their Creator with certain unalienable rights, that among these are Life, Liberty and the pursuit of Happiness.*

To this, Trump guffawed, saying, "Come on! How can you talk about freedom and that 'all men are created equal' stuff when you were a slave owner your entire life?!"

Jefferson hung his head. "I remain deeply troubled that I did little to diminish the grip-hold that the institution of slavery had on the economy of the colonies and on our young nation," he admitted. "But in my own defense, would you like to know a little detail about the Declaration few have heard? I know you love gossip as much as I!"

"Sure, spill it," said Trump, rubbing his diminutive palms together.

"Well," continued Jefferson, "The Second Continental Congress made over eighty-five edits to my glorious first draft of the Declaration. The most dis-

appointing to me was a quite poetic statement that I had penned condemning Britain's slave trade. It was removed only against my robust objections. It was an argument I simply could not win because the colonies allowed slavery and, remember, many of the founding fathers owned slaves."

Trump exclaimed "Ha! You know, speaking of founding fathers, I just spoke with Washington—who, by the way, now happens to be a great personal friend of mine—about how the so-called father of our country deplored partisanship and divisiveness. But not you Tommy! You and I must be cut from the same cloth. You might as well be known as the father of political parties!"

Jefferson acknowledged that he had been very partisan and had fought with John Adams and Alexander Hamilton constantly.

"It's true, Adams and I created very divisive political parties that entangled the country for decades," he said. "But really, Adams and Hamilton wanted a centralized government with its own bank! That might as well have been a monarchy!"

Jefferson continued with passion, "They grasped at supreme power, whilst I argued for much less stringent governmental controls. I believed that the individual should not be subservient to the state. The state should be subservient to her people."

Trump chuckled, "Let's face it, Tommy, you were a lifelong hypocrite! Not only did you own slaves, but you spearheaded a political party that split the country for more than two decades to keep its grip on power. I will say this, though, you may have been the

# IN CONGRESS, JULY 4, 1776.

## The unanimous Declaration of the thirteen united States of America.

most autocratic president of all time. So, you weren't all bad."

"Ah, Mr. President, you are referring to my campaign against the Barbary pirates and the Louisiana Purchase! Yes, I took it upon myself to build up the United States Navy and to expand the Marines. But you must understand, I wanted to earn the respect of seafaring nations. And it was only after my young nation alone crushed the Barbary pirate strongholds in the Battle of Derna, planting our flag in 1805, that America came to be respected on the high seas. Were you aware that the Marines' Hymn line 'to the shores of Tripoli' refers to the Barbary War? My Barbary War!

"And, of course, none truly regret my doubling the size of our young country through the Louisiana Purchase."

"I couldn't agree more. Bigger is always better," Trump interjected.

"Ah, so you admire that the purchase agreement I penned with Napoleon Bonaparte was at 'fire sale prices' because he desperately needed funds for his war in Europe?"

"Little Napoleon, huh? And they say *I* have foreign entanglements!" jeered Trump.

"I have had quite enough of your mocking ways, Mr. President," said Jefferson, turning up his nose. "I committed to Mr. Washington that I would try to help you for the sake of the nation, but we are hardly *simpatico*. Yes, when I had the chance to negotiate the Louisiana Purchase, I disregarded the Congress, and much of the citizenry, and moved to complete the sale independently. And I fully admit that I expanded my executive powers to conclude the deal with federal funds I had no right to access. In the end, though, Congress approved the Louisiana Purchase. But I would have done it regardless."

"It was a phenomenal deal," said Trump. "And I should know, I've done some of the most amazing real estate deals anybody's ever seen."

Jefferson buried his face in his hands. As the time to take leave of President Trump neared, Jefferson imparted these words to him: "My history has been written, but yours has not. Despite my own flaws, I accomplished much. And Mr. President, despite your…*many* flaws, you can still strive for a more honorable term in office. It is never too late. I can only hope that by opening my heart to you, I have helped to open your heart, your mind, and your eyes. Strive to be better, Sir."

Then the Sage of Monticello disappeared just as suddenly as he had appeared.

**PRESIDENTIAL CONVERSATIONS**

# JACKSON

# KING ANDREW
# THE FIRST

he portrait of Andrew Jackson by painter Ralph Eleaser Whiteside Earl, which Trump had prominently displayed in his Oval Office, suddenly came alive. And out stepped Old Hickory from the ornate gold frame.

The president was overjoyed. "Andy! My hero!" he exclaimed. Trump jumped out of his seat and, rather uncharacteristically, embraced this presidential visitor.

Jackson wrinkled his face into a fixed smile, saying, "I will allow the familiarity, though understand, Mr. President, as a former general, near emperor and man of the 19th century, I am not very receptive to such greetings. But as it is you, I can allow the familiarity and permit the physical contact."

Trump boomed, "Finally, Andrew Jackson! My favorite president! Hey, did you know they wanted to take you off the twenty-dollar bill? But I stopped them!"

Jackson nodded his approval and said, "Yes, I do appreciate that, Mr. President."

"No need to thank me," replied Trump. "This idea that one of our greatest *nonliving* presidents should be replaced on the most-used U.S. currency by... Harriet Tubman? I'm sure she was a very nice lady, but *no. No bueno.*"

"We are both known for our love of populism and for the steadfast devotion of our people," said Jackson.

"Not devotion...love," said Trump. "They love us, Andy, they really do."

"Except that I was elected to be the seventh president by winning the *popular* vote in *both* of my presidential elections," Jackson ribbed.

Trump bristled, "Yeah, well, when I was elected, there were more than three million illegal votes cast, at least that's what they tell me."

Jackson laughingly explained, "At least you knew better than to open the White House to the public as I did to celebrate my first victory. The interior of the White House was almost destroyed!

Now, I understand you are quite familiar with my many military campaigns and honors?"

"Sure, I know you are one of the most decorated military officers in American history. The Creek War, the Conquest of Florida, the War of 1812. And, of course, the Battle of New Orleans—that's the one that made you a national hero!"

"Sir, contrary to what I have been told, you *do* know your military history!" Jackson told Trump, who was radiant with pride. "I surmise your desire for military honors of your own is why you so often seek to associate with and surround yourself with generals and other decorated military leaders?"

"I was pretty decorated myself as a student at the New York Military Academy," responded Trump without a hint of irony. "You should see the medals I wore. I still have them in a box somewhere. Sometimes, when I'm by myself, I take them out, polish them up, and pin them on."

"I must admit, I find myself charmed by you," said Jackson. "And I know that you have come to practically idolize *me* for my reputation as a great populist. It is because I wish you well that I must warn you about the pitfalls of being elected more for personality than policies."

"I'm popular because of my policies," stammered Trump. "Who else is going to protect this great land from all the rapists and thugs trying to come across our borders? Why do you think it's so important to me to build that GREAT BIG BEAUTIFUL WALL?"

Jackson said, "I do appreciate how you seek to protect our country, but you must rethink how you go about doing that.

"I hope that sharing with you some of my poorer decisions will inspire you to be more cautious about your own decision-making. Perhaps you will even decide to change course.

"For example, I ordered the relocation of thousands of natives, driving them from the Southeast into less-settled territories like Oklahoma. History cruelly recast this brilliant and farseeing decision of mine as the 'Trail of Tears.'"

"Yeah, I heard about that," said the president. "The optics were horrible for you."

"So-called historians by and large failed to appreciate that I had vanquished the savage Indians to make room for Christian settlers. Nor have they appreciated how Southern plantations would not have flourished, nor would we have experienced the same cultural or economic boom, had I not shown such vision."

"I feel for you, Andy, I really do," said Trump. "I did the same thing throughout my career, so I understand. I took ugly, forgotten places—Atlantic City, for example—pushed out the people that couldn't add any classiness."

"You understand superbly, Mr. President!" Jackson exclaimed.

"Now, I do have one last piece of advice for you. Try not to be so pugilistic with Congress."

"I try, Andy, I really do," said Trump.

Jackson replied, "Try harder."

"You didn't have a speaker of the House like Nancy Pelosi to deal with!" Trump snapped. "I call her *Nervous Nancy*, you know."

"Perhaps you're the one who ought to be nervous now," quipped Jackson. "This constant boxing between you and Congress—well, between you and everybody—only adds to the divisions in the country. And it's not helping you. I *do* understand—we are similar, you and I. Like you, I never admitted mistakes or shortcomings until I was forced to."

"I never do," replied Trump.

"But Mr. President, I now see that I could have been better; I could have done better; we all can," Jackson told him. "I am strong enough to admit that. So, I beg of you, from one strong president to another, please recognize that pugilism for its own sake is not strength. There must be a purpose. You and I successfully appealed to the populace. You are correct to embrace populism, but you must act with national purpose to encourage *all the people* to follow you—not just your diehard supporters. It is only then that history may be written to show that you, too, did great things.

"Sadly, I must take my leave of you. I say this sincerely: I have met few men I would want as a brother. Be well, *be better*, and please, do not squander the love of the people."

As Jackson tilted his head, he morphed back into the painting. Trump called out, "No! Don't go! Stay!"

But the seventh president was gone; all that remained was his portrait.

PRESIDENTIAL CONVERSATIONS

LINCOLN

# THE PRAGMATIST

President Trump, still saddened to see Jackson depart, watched as Abraham Lincoln materialized.

"Lincoln!" Trump exclaimed. "Wow, you're even taller than me. I was just telling George Washington that people like having a tall president. They say you were also the greatest president—well, one of the greatest. But I have to hand it to you. You won the Civil War, you freed the slaves, and you were the first *Republican* president. Just incredible!"

"Well, it was quite a different Republican party," noted the 16th President, solemnly. "I see you were much taken by our presidential colleague, Andrew Jackson. Of course, you would be."

"Oh yeah," replied Trump. "Andy's a great guy."

"You and Jackson both delight in your populism and revel in your pugilism," said Lincoln. "You both may even believe that you are akin to an American Royalty. But President Trump, it is neither wealth, nor birthright, that provides strength of character, it is humility."

"What does that even mean?!," Trump wondered.

Not unkindly, Lincoln explained, "To be a masterful leader, one must first master one's own ego. That is what gave me the strength to lead in the face of so much tragedy.

"I could tell you about my humble beginnings; how I had to support myself; how I was determined to read and educate myself whenever I could. But I see from your expression that such stories do not move you. You may like this, however. Did you know that before becoming president, my only elective office had been to Congress? And that I had failed, twice in fact, to be elected to the United States Senate? Many believed I was ill-equipped to run the country."

"Me, too!" exclaimed Trump. "Way to show 'em, Abe! You and I have almost the exact same story! I had never been elected to anything. And I had never run anything but my businesses. And no one expected me to win the presidency, either. But never bet against Trump!"

"Please do at least acknowledge the differences in our beginnings and the opportunities afforded to each of us," implored Lincoln. "Furthermore, I had beaten three of the greatest political minds of my time, three of whom I appointed to my Cabinet—Attorney General Edward Bates, Secretary of the Treasury Salmon P. Chase, and Secretary of State William H. Seward. I knew I had no right to deprive the country of their service."

Trump bounced in his seat. "I did the same thing, Abe! Ask anybody. I put some of the men I ran against in my Cabinet! Best Cabinet ever, by the way!"

*FREEDOM* by Cleo

"I *listened* to my Cabinet, even if it meant having to make difficult, often excruciating decisions," replied Lincoln. "I sent men young and old to die for the cause of protecting our great nation.

Lincoln hung his head.

"My ledger of death included hundreds of thousands of men and boys," he said quietly. "I had to order them to die so that our nation might live. It was for the good of these United States that I sacrificed a generation of men. It was my will that set into motion the events of this hallowed chapter in our nation's history."

"Now that is true power," said Trump. "And it's what I try to project every day—just like you did."

"You talk of projecting power. You want to appear as if you have the strength of Samson," said Lincoln. "But I have observed you, and the seed of your strength is poisoned, for it does not derive from humility. Rather it is the act of a showman and it is empty.

"This great honor of serving as the president of the United States is not something you undertake for your own self-aggrandizement. Do you understand, Mr. Trump, that it was only through an act of sheer will that I convinced, practically forced, the Congress and my own Cabinet to agree to free the slaves? That it was only my 1863 Emancipation Proclamation that allowed all persons held as slaves be free?

"I assure you that I used every guile, every trick that I knew to effect our nation's historic emancipation."

"I'm doing the same thing!" declared Trump. "I'm using every guile, every trick in *my* book to try to save this country—not only from *Chi-na* and *Mex-i-co*, but from itself! But very weak and sometimes very bad people keep getting in my way."

Lincoln steadily continued, "I must try one last time. As you may know, I am perhaps best known for my 1863 Gettysburg Address, wherein I summed my beliefs in a simple passage.

*This nation, under God, shall have a new birth of freedom, and that government of the people, by the people, for the people shall not perish from the earth!*

"The decisions I made in wartime cost hundreds of thousands of people their lives. These decisions ultimately cost me my own life.

"I sincerely hope that by explaining the costs of my decisions and the pain that I carry, I have awakened you in some way. Please foster humility within in yourself and act for the good of all."

"You have such a way with words, Abe, just tremendous!" said Trump. "I can't wait to tell everybody about this! Trump and Lincoln together in the White House."

Before he even noticed this presidential oracle vanishing, Trump averted his attention to footsteps echoing in the opposite direction.

**PRESIDENTIAL CONVERSATIONS**

# JOHNSON

# THE FIRST
# IMPEACHMENT

he footsteps belonged to the red-faced Andrew Johnson, who entered in a flurry.

"Did I miss my cue?" he called out above him, to whom it was not entirely clear.

Johnson wiped beads of sweat from his brow, dusted off his overcoat and caught his breath. Then, with an oddly ceremonious bow, Lincoln's successor greeted President Trump.

"My apologies, President Trump," Johnson said. "But I always enter after Mr. Lincoln…leaves the stage."

"Is that some kind of sick joke, Johnson?" asked Trump.

Johnson looked down and nodded guiltily.

"Loser!" snapped Trump. "The only reason you were Lincoln's vice president was because as a Northern Republican, he needed a Southern Democrat for a 'unity ticket.'"

"Yes, that is true," admitted Johnson.

"And when you were sworn in as vice president, they say you were so drunk that you had to go into hiding to avoid public ridicule!"

"Yes, well, that rumor has persisted, hasn't it?" chortled Johnson. "Pardon me…"

Johnson then removed a small silver flask from his inner pocket and took a quick nip.

Trump scolded him, "Come on, Johnson, get it together. Do you realize how weak you look, you old wino?!"

"My dear sir, I never cared much for wine," Johnson stammered. "*Whiskey* has always been my preference. I may have enjoyed a sip or two of gin, but only in summertime."

"Let's face it, Johnson, you're a lost cause," said Trump. "When the presidency was handed to you—only because Lincoln was assassinated six weeks into his second term—you blew it! Some people say you were the *worst* president in American history."

"Yes, well, it appears that may be changing soon," quipped the 17th president.

"I attempted to create a lasting peace *and* to give back power to the Southern states. I permitted them to reelect 'secessionist' legislators and even let them pass 'black codes' to deprive the freedmen of their civil liberties. And yes, I did oppose the Fourteenth Amendment, which gave citizenship to former slaves."

"And the hits keep coming," Trump groaned.

"But I ultimately lost those battles, thanks to congressional Republicans. And even when I vetoed their bills, they would override my veto!

"The final indignity came when Congress passed the Tenure of Office Act in 1867 in order to stop me from dismissing Lincoln's holdover Cabinet officials. Naturally, I defied congress and dismissed Lincoln's Secretary of War, Edwin Stanton. As a result, I was impeached by the House of Representatives, and narrowly avoided conviction in the Senate and removal from office."

"Don't say that word!" said Trump. "*Impeachment* is a terrible, very nasty word. I hate that, because of the impeachment thing, I get lumped together with losers like you. And I don't like people comparing my executive orders to yours, I really don't.

"You are a real piece of work, Johnson. I'm insulted they sent you to talk to me."

"Be that as it may, Mr. Trump, remember, *I* was vindicated," Johnson snipped. "Five years after I left the presidency, I was elected to the United States Senate from Tennessee. May you be so lucky."

Trump replied. "Johnson, I've got two words for you: *You're fired.*"

And with that, Andrew Johnson was vanquished from Trump's Oval Office.

PRESIDENTIAL CONVERSATIONS

ROOSEVELT

# THE ENVIRONMENTAL WARRIOR

A loud *clomp, clomp, clomp* heralded the arrival of Teddy Roosevelt, who trotted in atop his horse, clad in his favorite "Rough Rider" uniform and looking every bit the hero of the Spanish-American War.

President Trump leapt up from his chair and yelled, "Teddy Roosevelt! Finally, a fellow president who I'm sure will make me feel good. I've been talking to some real downers! I have to tell you, you may be one of the few guys who can pull off a walrus mustache—unlike John Bolton."

Roosevelt hopped off his horse with aplomb and stomped right up to the president: "Sorry to disappoint you, Sir, but as you may know, I spoke very bluntly about my fellow presidents when I was alive—Taft and Wilson—and I see no reason not to continue that tradition."

Trump slumped over, visibly deflated. "Oh."

"You, sir, are full of flubdub. You love to play the tough guy. I saw your staged takedown of another suited businessman at a WWE wrestling match. But have you ever even been in a *real* fight?

Trump sucked in some air, then shook his head no.

"I will give you this, Trump: You have a true fighting spirit. But remember, it takes strength of mind, body and spirit to make the truly tough decisions."

"Yeah, okay, tough guy," snickered Trump.

Though much shorter than Trump, Roosevelt stood on tiptoe, pumped his chest, and came face to face with him.

"You bet I am," said Roosevelt. "I was born tough. I was a sickly child but defied all odds through sheer will. My successes were matched only by my drive and sprouted from the seed of grit.

"Yes, I am known as a writer, explorer and military leader; governor of New York; police commissioner of New York City—the youngest to be appointed; and at 42 years of age, I also became the youngest person to assume the presidency after President McKinley was assassinated.

"But the achievement of which I am most proud is my work as a conservationist and environmentalist. My efforts to preserve and protect this beautiful land of ours is my greatest legacy of all.

"I built the Panama Canal and passed the 1906 American Antiquities Act, which protected more precious lands than before or since. And I proudly, and famously, uttered these words.

*STRENGTH* by Cleo

*We have fallen heirs to the most glorious heritage a people ever received, and each one must do his part if we wish to show that the nation is worthy of its good fortune. ... It is also vandalism wantonly to destroy or to permit the destruction of what is beautiful in nature, whether it be a cliff, a forest, or a species of mammal or bird. Here in the United States we turn our rivers and streams into sewers and dumping-grounds. We pollute the air, we destroy forests and exterminate fishes, birds and mammals—not to speak of vulgarizing charming landscapes with hideous advertisements. But at last it looks as if our people were awakening.*

"And yet, despite the great strides that have been made, you, Trump, seek to roll back environmental protections—ignoring the scourge of climate change; allowing drilling in our parks and on our pristine coastlines; and the biggest personal effrontery of all, shrinking our national parks in the very parks system that I created!"

"Whatta you talking about, Teddy?" pleaded Trump. "I signed a bill protecting two million acres and created new parks!"

"A small gesture, Trump, you can do much more," Roosevelt replied. "Look what I did! My United States Forest Service protected 230 million acres of public land. Now that, good sir, in your parlance is what is known as a *huuuuuge* legacy."

Trump looked Roosevelt right in the eye, both their faces red with passion.

"That was a very long time ago, Teddy," Trump huffed. "And I've got my own very long list of very big accomplishments. I've opened up more land to oil and gas development than anybody. I ended the 'war on coal' to save jobs. I got us out of the Paris Agreement. I refused to cripple energy independence by trying to protect so-called Indian burial sites at the expense of building the Keystone pipeline—and let me tell you, it's a beautiful pipeline."

"Everything you just said is completely antithetical to my point!" hammered Roosevelt.

"The only thing I hate almost as much as fake news is bad science," Trump responded.

At this, Roosevelt threw up his hands and shouted, "You, Sir, are an utterly hopeless, utterly hapless soul!"

Trump reached out and condescendingly patted Roosevelt on the head, snickering, "Yeah, okay, *Teddy Bear*, whatever you say."

"Listen here, *Trumpie*," snapped Roosevelt. "I'll have you know that I once refused to shoot a baby bear on a hunting expedition and thus the term 'teddy bear' was born."

"I myself never cared for teddy bears, or stuffed toys of any kind," said Trump. "I always found them far too smoosh-y."

"May you be so lucky as to leave something behind to be beloved for generations," Roosevelt replied.

The Rough Rider then mounted his horse and said, "I can see my efforts with you have been in vain. But I do hope that you will reconsider some of your environmental policies and realize that business interests need not necessarily be advanced at the expense of conservation principles."

As Roosevelt's horse bellowed, he took hold of the reins and strode out, calling out behind him, "At least don't forget—and this should be easy enough for you to remember—when in doubt, better to speak softly and carry a big stick."

As the 26th president galloped off, vanishing into thin air, Trump could have sworn he heard music playing.

**PRESIDENTIAL CONVERSATIONS**

# HARDING
# COOLIDGE
# HOOVER

# THE ROARING TWENTIES REPUBLICAN TRIO

A microphone squeaked as an unseen announcer's voice echoed, "Take a seat, Mr. President. It's time for the musical entertainment portion of the evening to begin!"

"What the hell is this?" Trump thought to himself but obliged and sat down at his desk.

As a dramatic drumroll began, the announcer's voice boomed through unseen speakers, "Ladies and gentlemen—or just, *gentleman*, the White House Oval Office Stage is pleased to present The Roaring Twenties Republicans! Please give a warm welcome to everybody's favorite presidential singing trio! Warren Harding! Calvin Coolidge! *Aaand* Herbert Hoover!"

Upbeat jazz music swelled as Presidents Harding, Coolidge and Hoover entered from different directions, toe-tapping in sync up to their respective mics amid raucous applause from an unseen audience.

"Thank you! Thank you very much!" boomed Hoover's voice into the microphone. "It is our pleasure to be with you this evening!"

Harding chimed in, "They say our policies led to the Wall Street Crash of 1929—that's Black Tuesday for all you kiddies out there, the day it all came *crash-crash-crashing* down—and The Great Depression!"

"Don't forget now, we've got a very special man with us in the audience tonight!" cut in Coolidge. "So, without further ado: President Trump, our pro-business, anti-regulation, mass-production, scandal-plagued Republican comrade in arms—this one's for you!"

Trump beamed, tapping his fingers and toes in rhythm.

Harding counted them off: "*A-one, a-two, a-one-two-three-four.*" And the Roaring Twenties Republicans began harmonizing.

*Be aware*
*If you dare*
*That laissez-faire*
*Meant much to bear*
*'Cause we didn't care*
*Tha-a-a-a-at*
*Cutting-cutting-cutting*
*Taxes*
*(ka-ching!)*
*And cutting-cutting-cutting*
*Regs*
*(ka-ching!)*
*Would lead to*
*Crashing-crashing-crashing*

*Stocks*
*(ka-ching!)*
*And crying-crying-crying*
*Babies*
*(ka-ching!)*
*And hungry-hungry-hungry*
*Children*

Trump sang out, "KA-CHING!"

"That's it, Mr. President!" Coolidge cried out. "Now you've got it!"

Trump stormed the stage. "Hey fellas, what do you say we make this a *quartet?!*"

He began snapping his fingers in unison with the other three. A mic stand appeared out of nowhere and Trump crooned into the microphone, as Harding, Coolidge and Hoover sang backup.

*I've got the impeachment blues, baby*
*I've got the recession blues, baby*
*And the Covid blues, baby*
*My numbers are tanking*
*There goes my ranking*
*And Pelosi, man, she's really spanking*

Hoover gives Trump a playful smack on his bum.

*So, my bags I better start packing*
*(start-a-packing)*
*I guess we're gonna stop fracking*
*(stop-a-fracking)*
*It wasn't hubris that I was lacking*
*(was-a-lacking)*
*My god…I feel like…I'm…cracking!*

As Harding, Coolidge and Hoover sang *he's-a-cracking*, a garbled, distorted noise pierced through the speakers.

Trump shut his eyes, plugged his ears and yelled, "Make it stop!"

And he was suddenly alone again in the Oval Office. No singing. No music. And no Roaring Twenties Republican Trio.

PRESIDENTIAL CONVERSATIONS

ROOSEVELT

# THAT MAN IN THE WHITE HOUSE

car horn bugled, announcing the 32ⁿᵈ president, and in rode Franklin Delano Roosevelt atop a self-driving *Sunshine Special*, his beloved presidential convertible.

"Look at you! Roosevelt!" Trump exclaimed.

A refreshed-looking FDR hopped off the car, debonair in a white straw boater hat, wielding his famous silver cigarette holder.

"Mr. Trump, how do you do?"

"I'm fine, I'm great, but how about you?" replied Trump. "I've never seen you looking so young and healthy, standing so strong. I always think of you crumpled up in a wheelchair with a blanket over your knees."

"It's true," FDR said. "In life, I was saddled with an array of ailments, among them the polio that took my health and the use of my legs. But now, I'm full of vigor."

"Good. Does that mean you're going to be *nice* to me?" Trump asked.

FDR replied, "Well, let's just say you can't tame a tiger into a kitten by stroking it."

Trump leaned back, "Whoa, don't get any ideas!"

FDR threw his head back with a chuckle, then puffed on his cigarette.

"You really should quit," scolded Trump. "Smoking happens to be a horrible habit. I myself can't stand smoking, and I hate it when filthy smokers expect me to suck in their disgusting air. My personal physician is very happy that I don't smoke, and he tells me I am not only the healthiest man to ever serve as president, but also one of the healthiest, strongest and most virile men to ever walk the earth."

Hearing this forces FDR to cough, blowing out smoke.

"See, I told you," said a self-satisfied Trump.

"Perhaps there's something to what you say, Mr. Trump," admitted FDR. "My poor health, not to mention the stress of leading this country during two of the most tumultuous events of the 20th century— the Great Depression and the Second World War— contributed to my untimely death at only sixty-three years of age."

"Ha! When I was 63, I was starring on the number one TV show in America, which some people think is the greatest television show of all time. You may have heard of it? *The Apprentice*?"

"I see I have my work cut out for me," sighed FDR.

"Bring it on, I got no problems with that!" said Trump. "As you may have heard, I'm not so fond of

Democrats, but you're not so bad. They even say my rallies are like your fireside chats, but BIG."

"I appreciate that," replied FDR. "Especially since your conservative colleagues from my time had a not too flattering nickname for me—'that man in the White House.'"

"That's nothing," said Trump. "They call me 'that *orange* man in the White House!'"

"I know you have already been visited by other presidents this evening—" began FDR.

"Yeah," interjected Trump. "As a matter of fact, the other Roosevelt, Teddy, paid me a visit. What was he, your uncle or something?"

"Theodore was my fifth cousin," FDR replied. "In fact, I was related by blood to several other presidents: Adams; Madison; the other Adams, John Quincy; Van Buren; Harrison; Taylor; Johnson; Grant; Harrison; and Taft."

"Keeping it all in the family, eh?" Trump cracked. "I'm all for that!"

"So I've heard," FDR murmured.

Trump rattled off names, "The Roosevelts…the Rockefellers…the *Trumps*—all great American families!"

FDR continued, "I may have been born with the proverbial silver spoon—as were you."

Trump corrected him, "For me it was a *gold* spoon."

"Be that as it may," replied FDR, "as the oft-quoted saying goes, 'To whom much has been given much is expected.'

"Though I was greatly privileged, the terrible crippling disease from which I suffered instilled in me humility and empathy towards my fellow man. It helped me to understand the suffering around me. And I believe it greatly contributed to the spirit of liberalism with which I led. It also fortified me for the challenges I faced as president, having to make some of the hardest decisions any president had had to make and needing to create some of the most innovative government initiatives."

"They say your New Deal programs are what saved us," Trump responded. "And don't get me wrong, your New Deal was much better than this Green New Deal these whack jobs like Bernie and AOC are pushing now—but c'mon, your *deal* wasn't that *new* at all! You took Hoover's ideas to save American businesses and turned them into socialist giveaways!"

Roosevelt remarked, "Mr. Hoover indeed had his heart in the right place. But I alone had the strength of will to bend the federal government to save the country."

"*Bend?!*" taunted Trump. "Face it, Frankie, you did whatever the hell you wanted!"

FDR stiffened. "Like Lincoln during the Civil War, I knew that the depression confronting our people could undo the very framework of this great nation. So, I did what was necessary to create the kinds of public programs that would help people and put them back to work."

"What do they say? 'Scratch a liberal, find an autocrat,'" quipped Trump. "Relax! I'm not judging. I'm bending the government, too, every chance I get!"

*NO FEAR* by Cleo

"Do not compare us!" FDR stammered. "You rule by inspiring fear, whereas I sought to instill the opposite in our citizenry—from my very first inaugural address, when I proclaimed, *'The only thing we have to fear is fear itself.'*"

"You want us to think you were some kind of patriot," shot back Trump. "But we all know about your pork-barrel spending; and how you tried to pack the Supreme Court; and how you allowed the imprisonment of thousands of Japanese Americans in the aftermath of Pearl Harbor. And, Roosevelt, your New Deal wasn't what rescued the country from the Great Depression! I have it on very good authority that it was World War II and the wartime economy that did it!"

"There may be truth in what you say, Mr. Trump, but you have no regard for historical context. Do you realize what we were facing? It was upon *me* to foster America through her darkest days whilst the forces of fascism threatened our very existence at the hands of the most dangerous fascist leaders the world had ever seen."

"They weren't *that* bad," mumbled Trump.

"I am still saddened by some of the actions taken by my administration" continued FDR. "*Yes*, my clenching power may have stretched the bounds of constitutionality. And, *yes*, I may have attempted to pack, as you say, our United States Supreme Court with justices who would do my judicial bidding.

"Finally, *yes*, I allowed the Japanese internment camps in response to the country's ugly mood at the time, which may be the biggest stain on my presidency.

"But I wonder if you could have reforged the federal government in ways it had never been tasked to roll back the depression. I wonder if you would have had the strength to sustain our people after the seismic blow of Pearl Harbor. I wonder if you would have been able to march a war-averse, depression-weary country into a world war our nation had to fight. I wonder if you would have blinked in the face of facism or if you would have fought to defend America's freedom and preserve our standing in the world.

"You came to power in a time of peace. And yet you are abusing the power of this office and fostering divisiveness among the American people with your combative policies and inflammatory rhetoric.

"Please, for the sake of our people and the good of this country, I ask you to listen and learn from me and your other presidential compatriots."

"You know," Trump huffed. "I thought you were different from other Democrats, but it turns out you're all the same. You're just as shifty as Schiff."

"There is still time," FDR pleaded, as he began to fade from view.

"Yeah, I don't think so," said Trump. "I'm not gonna get four terms, like you did—although I'm sure people would like it."

Trump suddenly realized the Squire of Hyde Park had vanished, and once again he was all alone in the Oval Office.

PRESIDENTIAL CONVERSATIONS

EISENHOWER

# THE COMMANDER

A s Dwight David "Ike" Eisenhower marched in, Trump stood at attention and saluted.

Eisenhower saluted back and said, "At ease, Mr. President."

Trump loosened up and exclaimed, "What an honor!" Then he pulled back his suit jacket to reveal a vintage *I LIKE IKE* campaign button pinned to the inside pocket. "Look! I wear it sometimes—just on the inside."

"Will you look at that," chuckled Eisenhower. "I haven't seen one of those in quite some time."

Trump smiled, "What can I say? *I like Ike.* And I think you will like TRUMP."

"We'll see about that," said Eisenhower.

Trump marveled, "Look at you! The world's greatest general, who destroyed the Nazis and led America to victory in World War II!"

"Many people seem to be familiar with my war record, even now," Eisenhower replied. "But that's not what I came to talk to you about."

"No! C'mon, Ike! I wanna hear about D-Day! And Patton! And the German generals like Rommel!"

"Sir, I served our country in two great wars," Eisenhower told Trump. "But I have expressed my concerns about what I still consider to be a great scourge of our country: the military-industrial complex.

"Yes, we need a first-rate defense, but every arms dollar we spend above adequacy has a long-term weakening effect upon the nation and its security—not to mention the consequences of our getting involved in senseless, endless wars. I actually enjoyed watching you grill Jeb Bush during the 2016 campaign season over his family's disastrous foreign policy. It took guts to stand up on that stage in the GOP debates and take such a stand against what had become a sacred cow in certain Republican circles—the war in Iraq. That stance, however blunt you were in expressing it, really set you apart from your Republican opponents. What a sorry bunch they were. No wonder you won.

"Yeah, what a bunch of losers!" Trump boomed. "Not like me…and you…and Lincoln. We're *cool* Republicans!"

"Well, I wouldn't compare myself to Lincoln, Sir," cautioned Eisenhower, "and neither should you."

The 34th president pulled out a cigarette, lit it and inhaled, all in a single motion.

Trump wasn't about to protest. He detested being around anyone who smoked. But this wasn't anyone; this was IKE!

Eisenhower continued, "So, as I witnessed you ascend, my hope was that you would use that boldness with which you campaigned to address the runaway defense spending and unchecked growth of our vast military complex. But you have done just the opposite, boasting about how you've increased military spending in the trillions, far more than requested or needed. And you brought in warmongers like John Bolton—"

Trump interjected, "The Democrats actually supported my defense spending, can you believe it?! Only a few loons like Crazy Bernie Sanders opposed it. And don't mention John Bolton to me. I felt sorry for the guy because nobody in Washington likes him, so I gave him a chance. And this is how he repays me?!"

"You got any scotch?" Eisenhower asked.

"Sure, help yourself," said Trump, and a highball glass of scotch appeared at Eisenhower's hand. "None for me. I drink Diet Coke, but maybe tonight I'll have an Arnold Palmer. I know he was a golfing buddy of yours!

"Now what were we talking about?" continued Trump, changing the topic. "Oh, right. All the great Republicans, like me, you, Lincoln, Roosevelt, even Reagan. And just like you guys, *I'll* be reelected, too!"

At that, Eisenhower choked on his sip of scotch and cleared his throat. "Now, let's talk, president to president—"

"Commander in chief to commander in chief?!" begged Trump.

"I'm just hoping that perhaps I can get through to you, because we do have more in common than you may realize," Eisenhower said. "Like you, I wasn't a hardcore Republican most of my life; I pretty much stayed out of politics until I was elected president in 1952. In fact, four years earlier, in 1948, after our great victory in World War II, both the Republicans *and* Democrats wanted me to run as their presidential nominee. But, perhaps most important of all, you and I both presided over very healthy economies."

"And the Trump economy is going to come roaring back! You'll see, it won't be long! We're going to have the greatest economy of all time!" boasted Trump.

"For the sake of the people of this country, I hope that's true. But, as I was saying, I wanted to talk to you not about my war record but about what leading this country means. The call of duty oftentimes extends beyond the battlefield—for some of us, it even extends to this grand office. I was called to serve this country as its president, and so I grew into the kind of statesman that I hope made America as proud of me as I was to serve.

"I know I was proud to create the interstate highway system, one of the most ambitious domestic programs in our country's history, which sought to *unite* all the different parts of our country.

Ike continued, "And I was proud to sign the Civil Rights Act of 1957. In that same year, I sent federal troops—that's right, federal troops—to enforce the federal court's orders to integrate Central High School in Little Rock, Arkansas. I was also proud to continue the New Deal agencies; to expand Social Security; and to oppose Senator Joseph McCarthy's Red Scare under the guise of rooting out communism,

finally invoking executive privilege—coining the phrase 'executive privilege' in the process—to bring that *divisiveness* to an end."

"Executive privilege is a beautiful thing," Trump said solemnly. Then: "Hey, I've got an idea! You're our great golfer in chief, what do you say we grab our clubs and hit the White House green?!"

That was it. Trump had worked Eisenhower's last nerve. The former Army general visibly fumed as he realized just how futile his efforts had been.

"If this was the Army, you would have been dishonorably discharged by now, Mr. Trump," Eisenhower spewed. "But it's not, so that will be for the American people to decide."

"Aw, c'mon, Ike, I thought you liked me," said Trump. "Now can we please go play some golf? Maybe I can get Rudy Giuliani and Lindsey Graham to join us. Boy, would they get a kick out of seeing you!"

"I'll come back to tee off if and when you finally start taking this supreme command seriously," declared Eisenhower. "In the meantime, don't make me fire up my boilers!"

With that, President Dwight D. Eisenhower, also known as the Kansas Cyclone, whisked himself into an actual one-man twister and spun away into nothingness.

PRESIDENTIAL CONVERSATIONS

# KENNEDY

# THE
# LIONHEARTED

---

resident John. F. Kennedy strolled in next, beaming his unforgettable smile.

"Well, if it isn't JFK himself," Trump said, trying to look unimpressed.

Kennedy reached out his hand and greeted him in his trademark Boston brogue, "Good evening, Mr. Trump. It's nice to see you."

The 35th president of the United States took in his surroundings, saying, "And might I say, it's nice to be here again. You know, Jackie and I loved this place."

"Yeah, well we have our own Jackie O.," Trump said. "We call her Melania T."

"If I can ask you to refrain from referring to my wife as Jackie O. I'd appreciate it very much," Kennedy replied. "Besides, I didn't come here to discuss our first ladies' names, or nicknames, as it were."

"What did you wanna talk about, *Jack*?" asked Trump.

"In a word, I'd like to talk about courage," Kennedy said.

"Oh, right, like your book, *Profiles in Courage*."

"You know it?" Kennedy asked incredulously.

"Well, I haven't read it, but I've heard about it," Trump said. "I have a book, too. You probably know it? *The Art of the Deal*? It's a terrific book and one of the biggest bestsellers of all time. We did very well with that book. It made *a lot* of money for my publisher."

"Yes, well, the thing about courage is that you don't always know when you'll need it or even necessarily where it comes from," Kennedy continued. "Let me tell you a story about courage that's very personal to me—it was a baptism by fire, quite literally.

"I was 26 years old and a junior lieutenant in the Navy, captaining PT 109—an 80-foot torpedo boat, in case you're wondering—in the Solomon Islands in the South Pacific.

"It was 2:30 in the morning on a moonless night on August 1, 1943, when a 400-foot Japanese destroyer named the *Amagiri* collided right into us. She was running without lights, so we didn't even see her coming until our fuel tank exploded and our boat had been split in half. I lost two of my crew instantly. The rest of us clung to the half of the boat that hadn't sunk."

Kennedy became visibly emotional but remained strong.

"We held on for 11 hours, hoping to be rescued. When no one came to our aid, I decided that we had to make our way to the nearest island, which was three and a half miles away. One of my men was so badly burned that I had to clench the strap of his life vest with my teeth as we made our way to Plum Pudding Island.

"It took us four hours, because we didn't want to disturb the resident sharks or crocodiles, let alone the Japanese. From there, we moved to Olasana Island, where we survived for six days."

"Hey, is it true you wrote a rescue message on a coconut?" Trump asked.

Kennedy laughed and said, "Yes, that's actually true. There was a paper message as well, but I also scratched this onto a coconut: 11 ALIVE…NEED SMALL BOAT…KENNEDY. I gave both the note and the coconut to native coast watchers to take back to a U.S. military outpost. And we were rescued soon after."

Trump responded to Kennedy's poignant, dramatic tale, "That's some story. You know, I got a lot of great stories, too. Some of the most unbelievable stories you ever heard!"

"Thank you, Mr. Trump, but it's not the story that counts. In fact, on the campaign trail, they'd often yell out at me, 'Less profiles, more courage!' I told you that story not to impress you but to try to teach you. Recognizing in myself the ability to meet that challenge helped me gain the resolve to meet other challenges that came during my presidency, especially those 'Thirteen Days' in October 1962. The world was on the brink of a nuclear war as it awaited a peaceful resolution to the Cuban Missile Crisis."

"*Peaceful?*" snickered Trump. "Face it, Kennedy, after that Bay of Pigs fiasco, the missile crisis was your big chance to set things straight. People thought you were some peace-making president, but you and I both know what really happened down there in Cuba. In exchange for the Soviets removing their nuclear missiles, you allowed them to stay in Cuba. You let a foreign power—*Russia* no less!—have a foothold in the American hemisphere!"

Kennedy replied, "As you may recall, I told Americans in June 1963, 'Our most basic common link is that we all inhabit this small planet, we all breathe the same air. We all cherish our children's future, and we are all mortal.' So, of course I did what was necessary to protect America, the entire world in fact, from what could have escalated into a nuclear holocaust."

"I get it," snipped Trump. "You were trying to make America great—in your own way. At least you had some fun while you were in the White House, unlike some of these other guys. I mean, Lincoln for example? That guy needs to lighten up! Look at you, for instance. Not many men, whether they're the president or not, get to have Marilyn Monroe serenade them on their birthday, in *that dress*, right? Now that was a movie star! Not like some of these so-called actresses today, who spend more time busting my chops than they do making movies!"

Kennedy pleaded with him: "Mr. Trump, please, it's not all about *you*. Do you remember what I said in my inaugural address to this nation? 'Ask not what your country can do for you, but what *you* can do for

*COURAGE* by Cleo

your country.' You are the president; you could do so much!"

"Don't lecture me!" Trump snapped. "I've already been president for longer than you ever were. It wasn't your fault, but you gotta admit, it didn't exactly end well for ya.

"You know for a while there, during the 2016 election, I was trying to make the case that the father of Lyin' Ted Cruz—you know, the senator from Texas—was in cahoots with Lee Harvey Oswald. But I dropped it and now we're friends. Ted's a good guy.

"And by the way, speaking of that horrible day in November 1963, I announced that I was going to open all the JFK assassination records. But, believe me, you'll be happy I backtracked on that promise."

"You've backtracked on many of your promises," replied Kennedy.

"You know what, kid, Camelot is *over*, and it has been for a very long time," said Trump, as he walked up to the young Kennedy and popped him like an air bubble.

Trump continued chiding the empty space in front of him. "*You don't know jack.* There was never any Camelot in the first place."

PRESIDENTIAL CONVERSATIONS

# THE FATHER FIGURE

As the middle of the night wore on, Trump found himself having to wait awhile for his next visitor. He was hoping that it would be Richard Nixon.

Suddenly, the wall panels of the Oval Office separated and began rising into the air, like a theatrical set. Trump was now outside the White House, but everything around him was grainy and in soft focus. He felt like he was living in a home movie shot on an old 16 mm camera.

Nixon's 1972 custom Lincoln Continental limousine pulled up. The door opened and there he was! Trump's heart swelled.

"Nixon's the One!" shouted Trump, echoing the 1968 campaign slogan. Richard Nixon smiled and nodded, looking just as he did during the first term of his presidency. "Dick, I see you perfectly clear!"

Nixon waved Trump over saying, "Join me, Donald."

"Sure! Where we goin' Dick?"

"I'm taking you for a little joy ride," said the 37th president.

Trump stepped into the tricked-out limousine, and they were off! It felt more like they were floating than being driven. Indeed, Trump couldn't see who was in the front seat through the smoked glass partition. He assumed it was Manolo Sanchez, Nixon's long-serving valet, who was known for his unwavering devotion to his boss.

"Who you got driving this thing, Manolo?" Trump asked.

"Of course," replied Nixon. "Who else?"

"I need a Manolo," said Trump. "I bet he wouldn't try to peddle a book about me. You know how many books have been written about me, Dick? Probably thousands—more than any other president. I singlehandedly saved the publishing business. *And* the news business. I'll tell ya, there are a lot of awful, nasty people who work in those industries."

Nixon fumed, saying, "The media and the elites hated us *both*, Donald. I have *The Washington Post* to thank for taking down my presidency with their Watergate reporting. And did you see how the *New York Times* embarrassed me by publishing the Pentagon Papers?"

"The pricks. But you know what, Dick? I think they secretly love me. I'm good for business! As a matter of fact, I'm *great* for business."

"That may be, but you've got it even worse than I did, Donald. You've got a whole bunch of television networks that would love nothing more than to take you down. And from the looks of it, they're doing a pretty good job. But you're as tough as I am. You know this is a knife fight."

"This is a gunfight, Dick, and I'm even tougher than you were," said Trump. "You resigned. I never would have left."

"I would have been convicted in the Senate, and I knew it," said Nixon. "You knew the Senate would go your way. You had Senate Majority Leader Mitch McConnell—I didn't.

"Still, take my advice, don't let this ridiculous impeachment mark your place in history."

"I'm trying, Dick, I really am. I just want to make you proud. You know, you're one of my idols. It burns me up that you were always stuck in Kennedy's shadow!"

"Just like you are in Obama's!" Nixon added. "Damned prom kings! All flash, no substance."

"Guys like us, we're playing 3D chess while they're playing checkers!" Trump said.

"Damn right," huffed Nixon.

Trump beamed, "See, you understand!"

"Of course I do, son," Nixon said. "I mean. Well, er, I never had a son. But if I did, I'd want him to be a lot like you."

"Can I call you *Dad?* Just for the car ride?!" pleaded Trump.

"Well, I suppose so," Nixon mumbled.

Trump bounced in his seat excitedly.

"How great is it to be reunited like this?!" he exclaimed. "The last time I saw you was in 1989 at the '21' Club in Houston. We were dressed in tuxedos to celebrate the birthdays of the former governor of

Texas John Connally—Bankrupt John Connally—and his wife, Nellie. And you stole the show, playing 'Happy Birthday' on a white baby grand piano! Remember?!"

Nixon blushed. "Well, I wouldn't say I *stole the show…*"

"Yes, you did!" stammered Trump. "And then I flew you back to New York on my private jet."

Trump looked out the window at the D.C. skyline awash in retro-film graininess.

"Those were the days," he said. "And you know something else? I get a ton of letters from famous—I mean really famous—people. … We're talking kings and queens. But you know what may just be my favorite one?"

"Tell me," said Nixon.

"The one you sent me after you and your wife, Pat, saw me on the Phil Donahue Show back in 1987, I think it was. And you wrote that Pat predicts 'whether you decide to run for office or not, you'll be a *winner.*'"

"Well, truth be told, Donald," said Nixon. "I think Pat was a little smitten with you. You were a very nice-looking fellow."

"I gotta tell you, a lot of people say I still am," said Trump.

"Say, Donald, this is what I wanted to show you. Well, the first thing I wanted to show you."

Nixon cracked the window. "Have you ever seen the Lincoln Memorial at night?"

Trump smiled, "I've driven by it a bunch of times, but I've never actually looked at it…*Dad.*"

"Never forget the grandness of this monument, and of the man that it honors," Nixon said.

"Yeah, until they try to take it down," Trump replied. "Honestly, Dick, don't you think it would look better surrounded by our beautiful National Guard troops?"

"You know, Donald, if you're looking for a Republican president to emulate, perhaps you ought to consider this one. Not me."

Trump looked at him incredulously. "What are you, kidding me?! You were a *great* president. I mean, look at what you did opening up our relations with China. And what did they do? Stabbed us in the front *and* the back, and we let it happen! First with the bad trade deals then with this Wuhan flu. I call it the Chinese virus, but they tell me that's racist."

Nixon grabbed his attention.

"Donald, listen to me. I've had the opportunity to deliberate on a lot of matters. Like you, I was at the peak of my power, living my greatest fantasy. But I was taken down because of my hatred, paranoia even, about my enemies. Now your enemies are even fiercer than mine, which I never thought possible. But this country is so much bigger than our enemies list—"

"I don't know about that. Mine's pretty BIG," Trump interjected.

Nixon talked over him, "And the grandeur of this office is greater than either one of us, than both of us, frankly. So, there's one more monument I'd like you to see."

The presidential limo pulled into the Watergate complex. And there, right on the outdoor grounds, a statue instantly appeared. Trump stepped out of the car, looking up to take it all in.

"It's *huuuge*," he said.

It was a statue of Nixon, both arms raised, his hands in the famous V-for-victory gesture. At its base were inscribed the words he spoke on the eve of his resignation:

*Always remember, others may hate you, but those who hate you don't win unless you hate them, and then you destroy yourself.*

Trump turned back to get into the car, but it wasn't Nixon's limousine. It was his own. He looked over his shoulder, and Nixon's statue was gone, as was Nixon.

Trump stepped into the back seat and slammed the door.

"Take me home," he said quietly.

**PRESIDENTIAL CONVERSATIONS**

# CARTER

# THE HONORABLE MAN

immy Carter moseyed in next, wearing a denim shirt and blue jeans, with work boots and a fully outfitted tool belt, his hard hat emblazoned with the words Habitat for Humanity. He looked more like a construction foreman—a very *old* construction foreman—than a prior occupant of this grand office.

"Hey, this isn't where you want to be, buddy," Trump said affably. "The crew's upstairs, retrofitting the executive residence with all-gold fixtures—"

"Pardon?" a confused Carter said.

Trump had an easy rapport with construction workers, having worked with them since entering his father's real estate business in 1968. He extended his hand, "What's your name, Old Timer?"

"Why, I'm Jimmy Carter!" the 39th president replied with a broad, toothy smile.

"Jimmy Carter! It is you!" exclaimed Trump. "Geez, you've got to be 100!"

"I am only 95 years old, Sir," snipped Carter. "As one of the holders of this great office, I came to try to enlighten you, Mr. Trump. After all these years, I still want the same thing that I imagine—deep in your soul, *very* deep—that you want: a government that is as good and honest and decent and competent and compassionate and as filled with love as the American people."

"Enough with this mumbo jumbo, Jimmy! I'm really not in the mood," Trump huffed. "Besides, I'm not about to let a peanut farmer tell me how to run the country!"

Carter pleaded with him, "President Trump, there's nothing wrong with talking about things like honesty and decency and love—even when you're at the apex of power. Especially when you're at the apex of power. I must tell you, your presidency has been a downright disaster when it comes to human rights and morality."

"*You* are lecturing *me* about morality? Trump snickered. "Oh, that's rich coming from you!"

"Whatever do you mean?" Carter asked.

"Come on, Jimmy, you know what I'm talking about. Who's had *lust* in his heart, *hmmm*?" wondered Trump, citing Carter's infamous 1976 interview in *Playboy* magazine. In the piece, Carter admitted (rather innocently) that he had committed adultery in his heart by "looking on a lot of women with lust."

Carter hung his head in shame.

"Look, Jimmy, I'm sure you're a very nice man, but, let's face it, you were a very weak president," continued Trump. "You gave away the Middle East in the

*HONOR* by Cleo

Camp David Accords between Israel and Egypt—talk about the art of a *bad* deal!

"They criticize my 'American carnage' speech, which, by the way, was a very strong speech and was a hell of a lot better than your 'malaise' speech—the one where you said there was a 'crisis of confidence that strikes at the very heart and soul and spirit of our national will.' I mean, seriously?!

"The only reason there was a so-called *crisis of confidence* was because you were doing such a lousy job as president! You created double-digit inflation and a horrible recession with 22 percent interest rates! No wonder you ended up being a *one-termer*!"

"I'd be careful about using that expression if I were you," warned Carter.

"I've got three words for you, Jimbo: *Iran. Hostage. Crisis.* You lost Iran to Islamic nationalists. You allowed the U.S. Embassy to be taken over and Americans to be taken hostage in Tehran. And then, when you tried to fix it, you *failed* in your attempts to rescue them!"

Carter, trying to maintain his composure, responded, "The truth is, I brought civility and humanity back to foreign policy. America was America again. Now I know you love to criticize treaties without really understanding them, so let me educate you about something. The 1979 Egypt-Israel Peace Treaty not only ended a war, but it was also the first time an Arab state recognized Israel's right to exist. In fact, they awarded all of us the Nobel Peace Prize."

"Those things don't mean anything," sneered Trump. "Even Obama's got one!"

"You are a vulgar man," said Carter. "But you are the president, so Rosalynn and I will pray for you."

"You do that, Jimmy. I'll let everyone know you're praying for me," Trump replied, moving Carter toward the door.

"Yes, well, Rosalynn and I read Bible verses to each other every night—"

"That's great, Jimmy, watch your step."

"I do have one final request," Carter continued, as Trump escorted him out. "During the Black Lives Matter protest, you carried a Bible to St. John's Church across from the White House and held it up for all to see. I don't know if the Bible was yours or not; I imagine it wasn't. I know you don't care much for reading, but if you could just go to the Book of Matthew, chapter 5, verse 9—it's very short: 'Blessed are the peacemakers: for they shall be called the children of God—'"

"You got it Jimmy, thanks for stopping by," Trump said as he ushered the Man from Plains out of the Oval Office.

**PRESIDENTIAL CONVERSATIONS**

# REAGAN

# THE
# COMMUNICATOR

t didn't take long for Ronald Reagan to walk in, wearing that happy-go-lucky smile.

"Ronnie!" exclaimed Trump. "Finally, some star power. What a relief after that loser, Jimmy Carter!"

Trump shuddered.

"There you go again, Donald," Reagan said, shaking his head. "Negativity and put-downs haven't gotten you very far. And I'm afraid those things won't get us very far in our conversation tonight, either."

"I'm not being *negative*, I was just sayin' that Carter's a loser! I couldn't be more *positive* about your being here and those eight wonderful years you were in office. The Cold War was brewing…Wall Street was booming…not to mention those corporate tax cuts and all that deregulation—pretty terrific, if you ask me. Plus, that's when I began building my casino empire in Atlantic City! They say the TRUMP Taj Mahal was the most impressive hotel and casino ever imagined. Some people even thought it was a lot nicer than the original Taj Mahal—which, let's face it, could use a facelift.

"Ah, the '80s, those were the days," Trump sighed.

An enormous glass candy jar of vibrant-colored jellybeans suddenly appeared on the presidential desk.

"Mind if I help myself to some of these?" Reagan asked, grabbing a handful.

"Go right ahead, Ronnie, anything you want," Trump answered. "You know, I personally loved *Reaganomics*. I couldn't believe when 'Poppy' Bush—your own VP—referred to Reaganomics as 'voodoo economics.' What an idiot. And his sons? I'll tell ya, Ronnie, the apples didn't fall very from the tree there in that family."

Reagan started, "Donald—"

"Hey, *Ronald* and *Donald*! Two great presidents!" chimed Trump.

"Donald, I wanted to have a word with you about a couple of things," Reagan said. "You know, *I* was the one who said we ought to make America great again, back in 1980."

"Yeah, but you didn't have hats!" Trump shot back. "You missed a very big opportunity there, Ronnie."

"Let's try doing this a different way," Reagan offered. "Let me ask you a question. How do you see America?"

Trump squinted, saying, "I don't know what you mean."

"It's a simple question: *How do you see America?*" Reagan continued, "For instance, I've always thought of America as 'a shining city on a hill.'"

"I don't know; I never really thought about it," Trump said.

Reagan turned around and was suddenly bathed in white studio lights. Then he expertly addressed a television camera that had appeared out of nowhere.

*I've spoken of the shining city all my political life, but I don't know if I ever quite communicated what I saw when I said it....in my mind, it was a tall, proud city built on rocks stronger than oceans, wind-swept, God-blessed, and teeming with people of all kinds living in harmony and peace—a city with free ports that hummed with commerce and creativity, and if there had to be city walls, the walls had doors, and the doors were open to anyone with the will and the heart to get here. That's how I saw it, and see it still.*

"Doors??!!" yelled Trump. "I don't think so! Walls should not have any *doors*—are you nuts?! We have a very big immigration problem in this country. That's why I'm building a GREAT BIG BEAUTIFUL WALL. And I can tell you, there won't be any *doors* in my wall."

Reagan continued: "I received a letter from a man who explained how you can go to live in other countries like Japan, France, Germany or Turkey, but you cannot become Japanese, French, German or

Turkish. But anybody from any corner of the world can come to America to live and become an American, including those fleeing violent and oppressive regimes."

"You wanna talk about oppressive regimes, how 'bout we talk about *Nicaragua,* then?! Or *Iran*, as in the Iran-Contra scandal—you know, the not-so-secret little arms deal with Iran that almost brought down your presidency? You're lucky you were already into your second term."

"Well, you've got a point there, Donald," said Reagan, smiling affably.

"You were awfully friendly with that commie Mikhail Gorbachev, too, Ronnie. And they complain about me and Putin!" huffed Trump.

Reagan replied, "At the time, my talks with Mr. Gorbachev were crucial to maintaining peace between the United States and the Soviet Union, the global superpowers at the time."

"I'm not criticizing you, Ronnie! I love Russia!" exclaimed Trump. "You and I have a lot in common, no matter what the so-called Never Trumpers say. *You* loved space. *I* love space. As a matter of fact, they're saying the United Stated Space Force—which I started and which I wanted to call TRUMPFORCE, and still might—is one of the greatest things my administration, or *any* administration, has done. You did Star Wars, the Strategic Defense Initiative, but I gotta tell you, Ronnie, that was a horrible name. And a horrible movie, too."

"I must tell you, Donald, this meeting has tested even *my* optimistic resolve. On that note, I must leave you now. The other realm awaits—and so does Nancy."

Reagan reached up and took hold of an astronaut's helmet that suddenly appeared. He slipped it on and, with a twinkle in his eye, said, "One more thing, Donald. It may not look good for you right now, but, come the election, see what you can do to *win one for the Gipper.*"

Trump nodded, "I'll try, Ronnie."

Then the 40th president shot up into the endless sky in a cloud of rocket smoke.

PRESIDENTIAL CONVERSATIONS
CLINTON

# THE CO-
# PRESIDENTS

s the lights dimmed in the Oval Office, the sultry purring of a saxophone permeated the darkness. Spotlight on William Jefferson Clinton, wearing sunglasses and whistling into a shiny gold sax.

"Look at this guy," said Trump. "A bigger attention whore than me—well, almost."

When Bill finished his solo, he whipped off his shades and smiled to an unseen audience.

"Bill, you old dog!" Trump called out. "I'm actually glad to see you!"

"Hey, Don," Clinton replied in his unmistakable drawl. Then he approached Trump and used his tried-and-true right-hand handshake with left-hand shoulder grip combo before transitioning to a two-handed handshake.

"I've been watching your conversations with the other presidents," Clinton told him. "You must be feeling pretty beaten up. I know the feeling."

"I knew you'd understand, Bill!" nodded Trump. "We used to be friends, remember?! We were golf buddies. You came to my wedding when I married Melania. I supported both of your presidential campaigns. Hell, I even supported Hillary when she ran for the Senate!"

Clinton bit his lip and nodded "Yeah, but then it got ugly, Donnie. Real ugly."

"You mean 2016?! That was just politics!" exclaimed Trump. "Although it's no secret that I don't like your wife. She's some fighter, though, I'll give her that."

"Hey, Don?"

"Yeah?"

Clinton poked the air over Trump's shoulder, saying "She's right behind you."

Trump whipped around, and a look of terror overtook him. There was Hillary, seated at his desk.

"Surprise!" Hillary laughed uproariously. "Hiya, Donald!"

"Hillary?! What are you doing here?!"

"Well, my husband asked me to come along, and I thought, 'Why not?'"

Hillary leaned back in Trump's chair and, clad in a custom 'suffragette white' pantsuit, kicked her white pumps up on the desk.

"I could get used to this!" she beamed. "Come to think of it, this should probably be *my* desk and *my* office."

Trump groaned, "How is this happening?! Crooked Hillary, again?! I thought I was done with you!"

"This Crooked Hillary routine of yours is getting stale, Donald; I mean, it's not 2016 anymore. What are you going to do, *lock me up*?!" asked Hillary, throwing her head back in a fit of giggles.

"You're still the same nasty woman you always were," Trump chided. "It sure was sweet beating you at the ballot box."

"Well, technically, you didn't," said Hillary, collecting herself. "Remember, I won the popular vote by three million people."

"No! You! Didn't!" stammered Trump. "Somebody told me those were illegal votes. In fact, there's an argument to be made that *I* won the popular vote by the widest margin of victory ever!"

"There's no argument whatsoever to be made for that," countered Hillary. "Look, I'm not here to re-litigate 2016, Donald. I'm here to prepare you."

"For what?" demanded Trump.

"For life…as *a private citizen, ha, ha, ha,*" Hillary howled, cracking herself up. "Listen, losing is not so bad, Donald. It really frees up your time. Look at me, I've taken lots of walks, drunk some Chardonnay, and I've gotten to spend more time with my three precious grandchildren, Charlotte, Aidan, and…what's the other one's name, Bill?"

"Jasper," Clinton chimed in.

"Jasper, of course!" sang Hillary. "Beautiful baby Jasper."

"Hillary, you'll *never* be a part of this exclusive club of 45 *men* who have served as president of the United States," Trump declared.

"And you and I are in an even *more* exclusive club of just *three* men," Bill Clinton interjected, as he raised three fingers. "You. Me. Johnson. Impeached."

"No!" cried Trump, jumping up and down.

"Come on, Don, you've got to face it," said Clinton reassuringly. "That's why I agreed to visit you. I wanted to show that you can survive impeachment and still try to make yourself worthy of the office of the presidency, even try to make yourself a better man. Look at me—I've even given up our beloved McDonald's."

"No! No! No!" spewed Trump. "I don't wanna change. I don't wanna be a better man! I don't wanna be a vegan!"

"Take heart, Don," Clinton said, reassuringly. "You, me and Johnson may have been impeached by the House of Representatives, but we all survived trial in the United States Senate. You in particular were lucky the Republican-controlled Senate was so firmly ensconced in your pocket. Because it looked bad there for a while, Donnie, real bad.

"Johnson was fortunate because they didn't have TVs back then. You and I had no such luck. We had to endure this humiliation as part of the nonstop news cycle—"

"*Fake*-news cycle!" interjected Trump. "I didn't care. In fact, once I saw that the ratings were *unbelievable*, I welcomed it. I mean, the impeachment hearings numbers were through the roof! Some people said I was getting even bigger numbers than I got on *The Apprentice*, which were *huuuge*!

PRESIDENTIAL CONVERSATIONS
HILLARY

"Even FOX News said that impeachment was going to *help* me. I'd be able to say the socialist Democrats—like Nervous Nancy Pelosi and Shifty Adam Schiff and Nadler and Schumer—were just trying to reverse the 2016 election results, that this was a *coup* they were attempting. They even said, 'Look at what happened to Clinton; his polls went up!'"

"Don, I polled a lot higher than you to begin with," the 42nd president said. "Don't forget, I was a very popular president when the Monica Lewisnky scandal hit."

"Not more popular than Trump?!" Trump pleaded.

"I'm afraid so," said Clinton. "Look, Don, don't feel too bad. I don't think too many people could have survived everything you did. But every dog has its day. The Mueller investigation alone would have been curtains for most people, to say nothing of Ukrainegate *and* Covid-19 *and* the recession *and* the George Floyd protests and—"

"It can't be that bad, Bill, can it? Don't the people want to *Make America Great Again*?"

"Not this time, Donald!" cackled Hillary.

"Oh, geez, you again?!" Trump groaned. "Why did you bring her, Bill? You knew I wouldn't like it."

Hillary grabbed her husband's hand and gazed into his eyes. "We are *Stronger Together*…aren't we Bubba?"

Bill cooed, "We sure are, Hill'ry honey."

They nuzzled their noses in a sweet Eskimo kiss.

"Ewww!" Trump blurted out, "I'm gonna be sick!"

Bill Clinton turned back to him, "Listen, Don, I may not be a fan of how you've led this country. But I am firmly on the side of the office of the presidency and of this nation."

He turned to Hillary and smiled, saying, "We *both* are. And I want to believe that despite everything you've done in office, you still love your country."

"But just to be on the safe side, we're going to do everything we can to help make sure you are mercilessly annihilated at the polls on Election Day," Hillary added cheerfully.

"I hope that when it's time, you'll show some class and go quietly," Clinton continued. "And I hope these conversations with your presidential predecessors have at least inspired you to do that. Because Speaker Pelosi says she's certain you're going to challenge the election results if you lose."

"I'm not gonna lose!" countered Trump. "If it's a fair election, I'm gonna win and I'm gonna win BIG!"

Trump began frantically pacing in a circle, talking to himself, shutting out the Clintons.

"And by the time 2024 rolls around, maybe they'll change the rules because they'll want me back. Bloomberg did it in New York! He served *three* terms, and he's got nothing on Trump. Michael Bloomberg is a very small, very petty little man. Or maybe Ivanka will be elected next. She'll be the first female president, and I can stay in the Lincoln Bedroom. And she'll get reelected. Then who? Eric? Eh, probably not. Junior! Yeah, Junior. And then Barron. That kid's already taller than me! He'll make a great president, I'm gonna start calling Barron '48' from now on!"

Trump stopped in his tracks.

"Where'd they go?"

The Clintons were gone. Only the faint echo of Hillary's laughter remained, fading into the distance.

PRESIDENTIAL CONVERSATIONS

BUSH

# THE DECIDER

As George W. Bush ambled into the Oval Office, his boot spurs clinking, he tipped his oversize cowboy hat and greeted Trump in his clipped, Texan drawl. "Howdy, Trump!"

Trump narrowed his eyes and asked, "Did you bring Cheney with you?"

"You mean my 'ole VP, Dick Cheney?"

"That's exactly who I mean," replied Trump. "A lot of people say you don't do anything without him."

"No, Dick's not here, I'm ridin' solo this time," W continued. "Listen, Trump, we haf'ta talk."

"No, we don't *haf'ta talk*, Dubya. And knock it off with the cowboy act. I'm surprised you're not wearing chaps and wielding a lasso. Fact is, you and your family are WASPier than me!"

"Oh *alriiight*," said Bush 43, whipping off his 10-gallon hat and tossing it onto the desk.

"Now what do you want with me?" demanded Trump. "And why are *you* here instead of your father, President *H*.W. Bush?! I'm insulted."

"Sorry 'bout that. Poppy couldn't make it."

"Father-son presidents, imagine that," sniffed Trump. "Only the second time that's happened. The first was John Adams, who was a great president, and John Quincy Adams, who nobody cares about. But I can tell you, it won't be the last. I've got three sons just waiting in the wings. And I've got two daughters, too, who could become president one day, Ivanka and Tiffany. Well, maybe just *one* daughter.

"Everybody thought that if another Bush was going to get to be president, it was going be Jeb, not you. Oh, I'm sorry, I meant to say JEB! You know, I pummeled him, and all the other Republican candidates, too, in the debates for the party nomination in 2016."

"That is somethin', considering you're not even really a Republican," W replied.

"I'm more of a Republican and a better president than you were!"

"Listen, Trump," W continued. "I didn't come here to scold you or to try to compete. I just wanted to try to talk some sense into you about something that our Founders thought was very important. I'm talkin' about the separation of powers that's built into our government, so that neither the executive nor the legislative nor the judicial branch becomes too powerful."

"That's no contest, Dubya. Everybody knows that the executive branch is, by far, the best branch of government."

"Well, a lot of us think that you're endangering the whole system of checks and balances as well as the sanctity of the office of the presidency," W said.

"I mean, look at what you're doing with the judiciary and the United States Supreme Court, in particular."

"Whatya talking about?" stammered Trump. "I'm doing a great job! I've appointed more federal judges than any other Republican has in his first term! And I put two terrific justices on the Supreme Court, Neil Gorsuch and Brett Kavanaugh, who some people are saying may be the two best justices to ever serve on the United States Supreme Court. I've always believed in having friends in high places."

"Oh, come on," said W, "You can't expect every judge you appoint to do your bidding, just like you can't fight every subpoena from Congress."

"The hell I can't!" countered Trump.

"Then we're not living in a republic," replied W. "We're living in an autocracy."

Trump demurred, "Your words, not mine."

"It's not about having friends in high places or Republicans versus Democrat or staying in power at any cost."

"That's rich coming from you, Dubya! The only way you got to be president was because the Supreme Court was stacked in your favor with Republican appointments! They, very narrowly I might add, ruled in your favor in their landmark ruling *Bush v. Gore*, which pretty much decided the outcome of the 2000 election. It's a good thing Daddy sent James Baker to sort out that mess for you.

"Do I really have to remind you about that crazy election with the recount in Florida and all that business with the 'hanging chads.' *I* won Florida decisively in 2016, no questions asked."

"Yeah, better if you don't remind me," W shuddered.

"Don't get me wrong, I'm happy you ended up winning," Trump continued. "Al Gore may be tall, but he would have made a very bad president. Even worse than you. But you were pretty bad.

"You used the al-Qaeda attacks on September 11, 2001, to justify going to war with Afghanistan and then Iraq. Almost 20 years and it's still a mess over there. For what? So that you could avenge your daddy by killing off Saddam Hussein, then ride off into the sunset, like in some kind of demented spaghetti western?

"And look what's happened! The Middle East got even more destabilized. ISIS came to power—and they're even worse than al-Qaeda! Syria was pretty much destroyed, which caused thousands—no millions—of Syrians to flood into Europe, bringing their crime and drugs and Islamic terrorism with them. Just like the Mexicans are flooding our borders! That's why, wherever I go, they chant BUILD-THE-WALL! BUILD-THE-WALL!"

"You really don't get it, do you?" an exasperated W asked. "This kind of rhetoric hurts the country, and a lot of its citizens. Hell, we're a nation of immigrants!"

"Don't act like you were some kind of humanitarian president!" countered Trump. "Remember Hurricane Katrina? You treated the victims of Katrina horribly."

"No worse than you treated the victims of Hurricane Maria in Puerto Rico!" yelled W. "Listen, I wasn't perfect—"

"That's an understatement," muttered Trump.

"But why don't you try to learn from my mistakes?" W continued. "If you do, maybe *you, too,* can get a second term."

"You were *lucky* in 2004!" Trump shot back. "Senator John Kerry and his 'Boy Wonder' running mate Senator John Edwards were *losers*. People thought Edwards had great hair, but when the history books are written, they'll say TRUMP had the best hair in D.C. That's why you won't catch me dead in one of these!"

Trump pushed W's cowboy hat off the desk, and it vanished in midair. Trump looked around him. W was gone, too.

"Good riddance," Trump mumbled to himself.

**PRESIDENTIAL CONVERSATIONS**

OBAMA

# THE THINKER

When Trump turned around, he set his eyes on a fantastic sight. President Barack Obama was seated atop a marble pedestal, elbow on knee, chin in hand, like Rodin's sculptural masterpiece *The Thinker*.

Obama broke his pose, turning to Trump to greet him.

"Hello, Donald."

Trump sighed, "I can't believe I'm saying this, but I'm almost relieved to see you. You know, between me and you, I know I stir up a lot of anti-Obama this and anti-Obama that, but you weren't so bad."

"Well, I appreciate that Donald," replied the 44th president. "*Aaand* let me say that I am honored to sit with you again in this room. It feels like so much longer than the almost four years that have passed since we sat together in this Oval Office for the sacred ritual of outgoing and incoming presidents meeting to transition the governance of our country."

"You gave me some good pointers, O," said Trump. "I almost wish I would have listened to you. You're not gonna start yelling at me, too, are you?"

"Don't worry, Donald," Obama assured him. "Remember, I am uniquely qualified to understand the incredible weight of the presidency. You know the phrase, 'Uneasy lies the head that wears a crown?'"

"No, I'm not familiar with it."

"William Shakespeare?"

Trump responded, "Yeah, I always found Shakespeare highly overrated."

"What I'm saying is that I am not here to admonish you," Obama continued. "This is not an easy job, Donald. I'm well aware of that. That said, there has been a much higher number of, shall we say, *teachable moments* so far in your presidency."

"What do you mean?!" demanded Trump.

Obama furrowed his brow, "I'm not quite sure where to begin. For starters, I firmly believe that health care is a fundamental human right for all. And that is why, when I was elected in 2008 with Democratic majorities in both the House and Senate, one of my first orders of business was providing folks with health care."

"Obamacare sucks!" Trump exclaimed. "That's why I want to replace it with something much, much better. It's called TRUMPCARE. But so far Congress has not been at all cooperative."

Obama responded, "It feels to me as if you don't care as much about the policy as you do about putting your name on it."

*HOPE* by Cleo

"I resent that! Fact is, I've been doing a *great* job as president," Trump countered.

"Not from where I'm sitting," quipped Obama.

"Oh yeah, who could do better? You?! Joe Biden?!"

"*Weeell*, as of this Juneteenth, the polls certainly seem to reflect that the majority of Americans do believe that Joe Biden would do a better job as president," Obama pointed out.

"You can't believe the polls! They're put out by the Fake News Media!" yelled Trump.

"Actually, even FOX News has you trailing Biden," said Obama.

"Ever since they got rid of Roger Ailes, FOX News has gone way downhill! They might as well be a part of the Fake News Media now—except for Sean Hannity and a couple of others who happen to be very brilliant journalists.

"I just can't believe I have to run against *Joe Biden*," whined Trump. "They said it was going to be Crazy Bernie—"

Obama corrected him, "You mean Senator Bernie Sanders?"

Trump ignored him: "Or *Pocahontas*—"

Obama again corrected him, "You mean Senator Elizabeth Warren?"

Trump again ignored him, saying, "Nobody wanted *Biden!*"

"Well, apparently they did, since it appears he will be our party's nominee," said Obama.

"Yeah, don't count on it," sneered Trump. "The guy doesn't even know he's alive! Oh, geez, don't tell me *he's* coming to visit me, too?!"

Obama replied, "Oh no, there are no plans for Joe to visit you. At least…not yet."

"What do you mean *not yet*?" Trump asked.

Obama had a twinkle in his eye.

# EPILOGUE

The room started spinning. Once again, Trump was enveloped in a kaleidoscopic whirl of colors. He drifted through time and space, buoyed by a transcendental wave of energy. Was this the changing tide of history, he wondered. He had heard about it but never experienced it himself.

Calendar pages floated by, faster and faster, ticking off the days until the presidential election. The dates breezed past November 3, 2020, into December, then January.

Suddenly, with an unceremonious THUD, it all came to a stop. It was January 20, 2021, Inauguration Day. And Trump couldn't believe who was being sworn in as president of the United States.

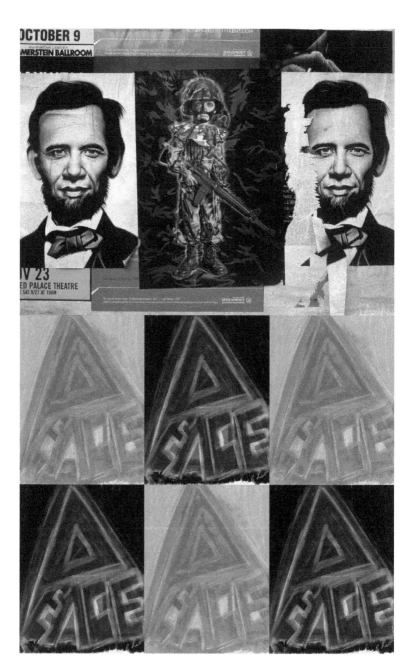

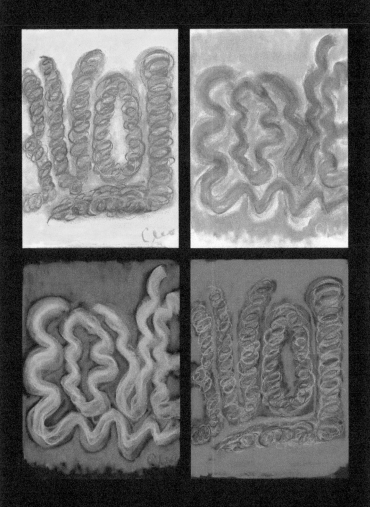

*LOVE* by Cleo

# AFTERWORD

My political awakening occurred in November 1972. During a vigorous pine tree apple fight behind Our Lady Queen of Peace grade school in Galveston, Texas, I attempted to explain to my fourth-grade classmates Richard Nixon's landslide re-election victory over George McGovern. My family had immigrated to the United States from Lebanon only a few years before, in 1968, when I was 5 years old, travelling by Pan Am Airways to a new world and new life.

Politics was an ever-present discussion topic in my family. Both my younger brothers were born in the United States and, as they like to remind me, *they* can be president and I cannot! But my family history was poignant. My parents and grandparents would tell us boys their stories about living under autocrats in Egypt in the 1950s and early '60s, until it became unbearable and they (taking their newborn boy, me) had to "flee under the cover of night," leaving their homes and businesses behind.

They would tell us that they tried to reestablish their lives in Beirut, and could have stayed, but that they all took a chance and our entire family moved from Lebanon to settle in America.

I had happy early memories in Beirut, from playing in the Mediterranean Sea to hiking around the Roman ruins at Baalbek and skiing in the mountains around Beirut. With the naiveté of a 5-year-old, I even found it thrilling to watch Israeli military planes fly over our apartment building during the Arab-Israeli Six-Day War in June 1967. After that, my family was ready to leave the Middle East.

We became U.S. citizens in 1972, and I insisted on signing my own name and raising my own hand in pledging to "support and defend the Constitution and laws of the United States of America." This was an especially formative experience for me, something the federal judge who administered the oath took pleasure in discussing with me after my swearing-in as a U.S. citizen.

My childhood in America continued to be shaped by the extraordinary political events of the time. I was glued to the TV set during the Watergate hearings during the fall of 1973 and spring of 1974. I was fortunate to have a sixth-grade history teacher who insisted on teaching her young pupils as if we were young adults. By junior high school, I had to be disciplined by the principal after I wrote "Carter sucks peanuts" on my homeroom chalkboard the day after Jimmy Carter defeated Gerald Ford for the U.S. presidency in November 1976.

Sensing my appetite for politics, the same principal began engaging me in discussions about political theory. These lessons challenged and expanded my mind.

In the many years since I've followed in the footsteps of my family members with their stories and of my teachers with their lessons. I have taken great pride in drawing my (14!) nieces and nephews into discussions about history and current events to help develop their own political awareness during these confusing and troubling times. And these discussions have helped me to articulate my own views as well.

But the greatest influence on me has been my wife, Cynthia. Not just because we experienced over 30 years of American politics side by side, but also because Cynthia, who is also a lawyer, was always an accomplished student of political science. Her knowledge of British and U.S. policies in the Middle East has deeply shaped my understanding of my own family history, as well as the basis of our strongly pro-British and pro-American views.

From all these experiences, influences and motivations, I thought to synthesize and summarize a book that could speak to all readers, including young adults, the way I speak to my nieces and nephews and the way my older family members and teachers spoke to me.

This book is a satiric imagining of fictional meetings between the 45th president, Donald J. Trump, and several of his predecessors. I thought this would be an educational and entertaining way to "examine, compare and contrast" the character traits of our 45th president with others, most of whom were honorable, to illustrate how the 45th president could "be better." Most of all, I hope this book spurs conversations about the presidency between and among readers of every political stripe, young and old, who can be encouraged to believe that the office of the U.S. presidency's greatest days may yet be ahead.

*George S. Corey*
*Washington, D.C.*

VOTE by Cleo

# ACKNOWLEDGMENTS

I want to thank my family and friends, who have given me love and support as I wrote this book, especially my team of young adult readers, who have provided much needed input and, hopefully, street cred too. My heartfelt thanks to my wife, Cynthia, for being my sounding board and inspiration; to the artist, Cleo, for her beautiful contributions to the book; and finally, to my publishers, Ken Siman, Benjamin Alfonsi and Christian Alfonsi at Metabook, who believed in *Presidential Conversations* from day one.

# ABOUT THE AUTHOR

George S. Corey is an attorney and lifelong student of presidential politics and personalities. *Presidential Conversations* is his first work of fiction. He lives in Washington, D.C. with his wife Cynthia, also an attorney.

Editor: Ken Siman
Creative Director: Benjamin Alfonsi
Art Director: Jason Snyder
Copy Editor: Gilbert Dunkley
Book layout and design: Erik Christopher
Photo finishing and design: Jackie Burwood
Image compositing: Yoni Weiss
Cover design by Benjamin Alfonsi and Jason Snyder

All original art by the artist Cleo
Photo of the author as a child courtesy of George S. Corey

*Obama Lincoln and Combat Clown*, Ron English, Lower East
Side, New York City, 2008, photo courtesy of Hank O'Neal

Colorful twisting psychedelic background and psychedelic
burst background by Robin Olimb, courtesy of iStock Photo by
Getty Images. Sprayed king font graffiti with overspray, vector
graffiti art illustration by Carabus, courtesy of Shutterstock.
Red, white and blue color burst copyright Mykola Lytvynenko,
courtesy of Dreamstime Stock Photos. Creative illustration of
no signal TV test pattern background, television screen error,
SMPTE color bars technical problems, abstract concept graph-
ic element, courtesy of Dreamstime Stock Photos.

Official White House portrait of Donald J. Trump by Shealah
Craighead, 2017; Portrait of George Washington, oil on canvas,
by Gilbert Stuart, 1796; *Parson Weems' Fable* by Grant Wood,
1939; Portrait of Thomas Jefferson, oil on canvas, by Rem-
brandt Peale, 1800; Image of The United States Declaration of
Independence is a version of the 1823 William Stone facsimile;
*Writing the Declaration of Independence, 1776*, painting by Jean
Leon Gerome Ferris, from the Virginia Historical Society, date
unknown; Stone drawing of Andrew Jackson by Jean-Baptiste
Adolphe Lafosse, 1856, based on daguerreotype by Matthew
Brady; King Andrew political cartoon from anonymous artist,
circa 1832; Matte collodion print by Moses Parker Rice based
on photograph of Abraham Lincoln taken by Alexander Gard-
ner, 1863; Image of the Emancipation Proclamation is from

the United States Library of Congress's Prints and Photographs division; Photograph of Andrew Johnson taken by Matthew Brady, 1875 or before, from the Brady-Handy collection at the Library of Congress; Photograph of Theodore Roosevelt taken by George Prince, 1904; Photograph of U.S. Senator (later President) Warren G. Harding, 1921, copyright by Moffett, Chicago, U.S. Copyright Office; Photograph of Calvin Coolidge, unknown author, 1923; Photograph of Herbert Hoover, Underwood & Underwood, Washington, 1928; Photograph of Franklin Delano Roosevelt, author unknown, 1933, from the Library of Congress; Official portrait of Dwight D. Eisenhower, 1959, Eisenhower Presidential Library; Dwight D. Eisenhower presidential campaign, Baltimore, Maryland, September 1952; Photo portrait of John F. Kennedy, White House Press Office, 1961, from the John F. Kennedy Presidential Library and Museum; Official portrait of Richard Nixon, author unknown, between circa 1969 and circa 1974, National Archives and Records Administration; Richard M. Nixon Campaign, 1968, National Archives and Records Administration, photo by Oliver F. Atkins; Photograph of Jimmy Carter, Department of Navy, Naval Photographic Center, 1977; Official portrait of Ronald Reagan, author unknown, 1981 (or 1983); Ronald Reagan holding "The Gipper" jersey at campaign rally in New York, 1984, Reagan Presidential Library, author unknown; Official White House photo of Bill Clinton, Bob McNeely, The White House, 1993; Official portrait of Secretary of State Hillary Clinton, United States Department of State, 2009; Official portrait of George W. Bush, White House photo by Eric Draper, 2003; Official portrait of Barack Obama, White House photo by Pete Souza, 2012; Sitting President and President-elect, Barack Obama and Donald Trump in the Oval Office, November 10, 2016, photo by Pete Souza.

CPSIA information can be obtained
at www.ICGtesting.com
Printed in the USA
LVHW071622151020
668918LV00028B/559/J

9 780999 211908